Kittens in 3-D

Kittens in 3-D
Copyright © 2010 GENKOSHA Co.

First Japanese edition published in 2010 by
GENKOSHA Co., Tokyo Japan

HarperCollins books may be purchased for educational, business, or sales promotional use. For information, please write: Special Markets Department, HarperCollins*Publishers*, 10 East 53rd Street, New York, NY 10022.

First english edition published in 2011 by:
Harper Design
An Imprint of HarperCollins*Publishers*
10 East 53rd Street
New York, NY 10022
Tel: (212) 207-7000
Fax: (212) 207-7654
harperdesign@harpercollins.com
www.harpercollins.com
Through the rights and production arrangement of Rico Komanoya, ricorico, Tokyo, Japan.

Distributed throughout the world by:
HarperCollins*Publishers*
10 East 53rd Street
New York, NY 10022
Tel: (212) 207-7000
Fax: (212) 207-7654

Photographs: Yoneo Morita (noa noa)
Photography assistants: Naomi Shirakawa, Yoshimi Toyoda
Illustration: Tsuyuko Tamai
Editorial cooperation: Little Dog (Moriya), Yuriko Sugiyama, Akikne Hirasaka, Kenji Kitami, Akira Hiba, Yoichi Yonemura, Noboru Yoshida, Hiroyuki Hayashi, Noriko Hirayama, Naohisa Yoshifuji, Kenji Kaneko, Takahiro Yamagishi, Gyoko Torai, Mio Honda, Minako Sakuma, Yoshie Fukatani, Midori Takeda, Mari Akimoto, Kyoko Suzuki, Minoru Yamazaki, Kaoru Sato, Yumiko Muramatsu, Reiko Nagao, and Natsumi Kuwabara
English translation: Kayoko Kimata
English translation/copy-editing: Alma Reyes (ricorico)
Book design and art direction: Makoto Tamaki (Erg), Andrew Pothecary (forbiddencolour)
Editor: Akira Fujii
Chief editor and production: Rico Komanoya (ricorico)

ISBN: 978-0-06-203957-6

Library of Congress Control Number: 2011921222

Printed in China by Everbest Printing Co., Ltd.

First Printing, 2011

Kittens in 3-D

Yoneo Morita

HARPER
DESIGN

An Imprint of HarperCollinsPublishers

Contents

Russian Blue

British shorthair

Using the
3-D Viewer

3-D Viewing Technique

Pictures with the **3-D** mark can be viewed three-dimensionally using the 3-D viewer. The distance between the 3-D viewer and the pictures should be around 7.5-12 inches; however, this varies per person. If you are not able to see the pictures in 3-D, try to adjust the distance between the viewer and the pictures while keeping the 3-D viewer close to your face. For pages with three images next to each other, the center image is viewed in 3-D. Focus on the center image and adjust the distance between the viewer and the picture. You can find the appropriate focal point and 3-D effect that suits you.

Using the 3-D viewer may cause eye fatigue. Avoid using it for long hours.

Viewing Kittens in 3-D

Everyone loves kittens. What better way to view them than in 3-D? The three-dimensional plane makes it look as though these playful kittens are jumping off the page and into your hand for a snuggle.

Images with the **3-D** mark give you an up-close-and-personal glimpse at these kittens' adorable features —their pink noses and tongue and softer than soft fur. In 3-D, these kittens are beyond cute! Enjoy!

Scottish Fold

The Scottish Fold is popularly known for its round-shaped face. The secret of its lovely feature lies in its ears, which point downward and lie flat over the head. This kitten has a mild personality and wide, innocent-looking eyes.

"I wish there to be in my house:
A woman possessing reason,
A cat among books passing by,
Friends for every season
Lacking whom I'm barely alive."

— *Guillaume Apollinaire,*
"The Cat"

"The trouble with a kitten is THAT
Eventually it becomes a CAT."

– *Ogden Nash*

American Shorthair

The ancestors of the American Shorthair were colonists that occupied the American continents. This cat was originally called a Shorthair; its name was changed in 1965. A working cat, it was primarily used to chase rats away. People have long appreciated the American Shorthair for its lovely appearance, beautiful fur, and personality. Over the years, it has become a popular breed and pet.

"The smallest feline is a masterpiece."

– *Leonardo da Vinci*

3-D

A cat's a cat and that's that.

– American proverb

Munchkin

This cat has short legs and is the feline version of a Dachshund. It originated in 1983 from a male cat whose legs were extremely short. At that time, people speculated that this kind of cat might have had a defective spinal marrow or bone structure; however, today, no problems are found in the cat's limbs. This cat has a very playful and cheerful character, and is considered one of the best breeds to keep as a pet.

The Timeline of a Munchkin

3 days old

7 days old

16 days old

48 days old

"There are no ordinary cats."

— *Colette*

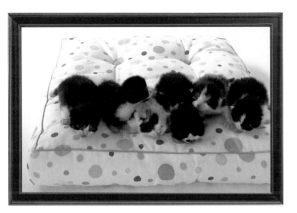

Munchkin

Russian Blue

This kitten is referred to as a "Russian aristocrat," with its short and blue-gray fur and green eyes. It is also called the "spirit of winter." Its ancestors were the result of Siamese and Russian crossbreeding. Presently, it is raised in England. A quiet kitten, it has also been called the "voiceless cat."

A dog may be wonderful prose,
but only the cat is poetry.

– French proverb

Russian Blue

Maine Coon

The prominent characteristic of the Maine Coon is its luxuriously thick, long hair. The frills around its chest and the volume of its tail are also charming. Its eyes droop ever so slightly; its ears are large and fringed with long eyelashes; its legs are strong and sturdy. A most unusual cat, its distinctive physical characteristics are matched by its friendly disposition and keen intelligence.

"Come, superb cat, to my amorous heart;
Hold back the talons of your paws,
Let me gaze into your beautiful eyes
Of metal and agate..."

– Charles Pierre Baudelaire, "The Cat"

"There were once two cats of Kilkenny.

Each thought there was one cat too many;

So they fought and they fit,

And they scratched and they bit,

Till, excepting their nails,

And the tips of their tails,

Instead of two cats, there weren't any."

– *Mother Goose, "The Kilkenny Cats"*

Maine Coon

Beware of people who dislike cats.

– Irish proverb

Abyssinian

The Abyssinan, true to its name, originally hailed from Abyssinia, the old kingdom of Ethiopia. Ancient Egyptians painted this cat's likeness on walls. This breed has an elegant figure; its legs are slender in proportion to the body. Despite its fine and delicate bone structure, this cat has a wild nature. The color of this cat's coat is unique, due to one dominant mutant gene known as Ta. The hair is a lighter color at the root and darker at the tip. The coat seemingly changes color before your eyes.

"If man could be crossed with the cat, it would improve man but deteriorate the cat."

— *Mark Twain*

Abyssinian

"First, I purred, then I discovered that inimitable talent of waving my tail in the most graceful of coils, and then the wonderful gift of expressing joy, pain, delight and rapture, terror and despair, in short, all feelings and passions in their every nuance with the single little word, 'Miaow!'"

– *E.T.A. Hoffmann*, The Life and Opinions of the Tomcat Murr

Ragdoll

This breed is known for its striking blue eyes, its distinct colorpoint coat, and its large body. The name "Ragdoll" is a playful reference to the fact that this breed tends to go limp and completely relaxed when it is picked up.

"I remained dumb-struck with pure awe. Reflecting, however, that I might get into trouble if I failed to exchange civilities, I answered frigidly, with a false *sang froid* as cold as I could make it, 'I, sir, am a cat. I have as yet no name.' My heart at that moment was beating a great deal than usual."

— *Natsume Soseki*, I Am a Cat

"'All right,' said the Cat; and this time it vanished quite slowly, beginning with the end of the tail, and ending with the grin, which remained some time after the rest of it had gone."

– *Lewis Carroll,* Alice's Adventures in Wonderland

Somali

The Somali is a slender, long-haired version of the Abyssinian. As it grows older, its huge tail becomes more elegant, distinguishing itself more clearly from the Abyssinian. It is very active, loves to play, and jumps and runs excessively.

Pussy cat, pussy cat, where have you been?
I've been to London to look at the queen.
Pussy cat, pussy cat, what did you there?
I frightened a little mouse under the chair.

– Mother Goose nursery rhyme

Somali

Somali

"The cat is a dilettante in fur."

– *Théophile Gautier*

British Shorthair

The British Shorthair, like its American counterpart, is known for chasing
away mice. As its name implies, this breed originally had a blue coat.
Today, its coat varies in color. Similarly, its coat was originally very short;
today, it can be quite long. Nevertheless, long fur or short, blue or brown,
this cat is a beloved pet.

British Shorthair

Persian

The Persian, also known as the Chinchilla, has very elegant and beautiful fur. It is said to be a masterpiece creation originating from Afghanistan, though there are various opinions about its true origin, which makes it very mysterious indeed. Its flat features, pretty round eyes, and gentle character make it adored by many.

"Whenever he found himself alone, he drew cats. He drew them on the margins of the priest's books, and on all the screens of the temple, and on the walls, and on the pillars. Several times the priest told him this was not right; but he did not stop drawing cats. He drew them because he could not really help it."

– Lafcadio Hearn, Japanese Fairy Tales: *"The Boy Who Drew Cats"*

Persian

Crossbreed Cats

Crossbreeds are pedigree cats that have parents from two different pedigree breeds. These cats are carefully crossbred considering distinct characteristics of each pedigree parent. A Somalian cat can mate with a Siamese cat; a Maine Coon cat with a Persian cat, and so on, producing offspring that display features of both parent breeds.

Two Methods of Using Autostereoscopic Vision

A 3-D viewer is attached to this book to help you obtain stereoscopic vision. However, even without this special viewer, you can also obtain autostereoscopic vision, which may require practice to use. Autostereoscopic vision does not require the use of any tool, and can be applied through two methods: parallel method and cross method.

   If you master the cross method, you will be able to see large images in autostereoscopic view, and be able to feel the power in the pictures' sharpness. (The images shown on pages 82 and 83 are viewed by autostereoscopic vision using the cross method.)

   Furthermore, autostereoscopic vision allows you to move the muscles around your eyeballs, which helps to correct nearsightedness.

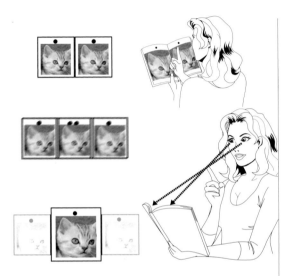 

Cross Method (Refer to pages 82 and 83.)

1. Look at the black circle mark ● above the images on pages 82 and 83.
2. As shown in the illustration above, place your finger at the center of the book and bring the book toward your face gradually.
3. As you focus your eyes on your fingers, you will become cross-eyed automatically. If you move your eyes from your fingers to the image, your right eye catches the left image, and your left eye catches the right image.
4. The image that appears between the left and right images is the stereoscopic image, which is formed mentally. This method may be comparatively difficult to learn, but once you master the technique, you can apply this cross method in time.

Parallel Method (Refer to page 85.)

1. Bring the book toward your face while looking at the red circle mark ◎ above the images on page 85. While doing this, you would be conscious about seeing the right image with your right eye, and the left image image with your left eye. Now, try to look at images in a distance, and not nearby. When you look at something nearby, you tend to be cross-eyed spontaneously. But, this does not mean your right eye sees the right image, or your left eye sees the left image. Try to practice this method by looking at something in a distance away from the book.
2. When you look closely at the images in the book, your focus becomes blurry and the red circle mark ◎ becomes naturally out of focus. Also, you begin to see three or four overlapping and blurry red circle marks ◎. If you see four red circles ◎, maintain this position by leaning your head sideways until you can see three red circles ◎.
3. Move your face away from the book gradually while keeping this position to see three red circles ◎. Then, focus on both the right and left images, and a new image appears between them. The new image is stereoscopic image, which is formed mentally. It may be comparatively easy to learn this parallel method for viewing images in 3-D.

"That way look, my Infant, lo!
What a pretty baby-show!
See the Kitten on the wall,
Sporting with the leaves that fall,
Withered leaves—one—two—and three—
From the lofty elder-tree!
Through the calm and frosty air
Of this morning bright and fair,
Eddying round and round they sink
Softly, slowly: one might think,
From the motions that are made,
Every little leaf conveyed
Sylph or Faery hither tending,—
To this lower world descending,
Each invisible and mute,
In his wavering parachute.

But the Kitten, how she starts,
Crouches, stretches, paws, and darts!
First at one, and then its fellow
Just as light and just as yellow;
There are many now—now one—
Now they stop and there are none."

– *William Wordsworth, excerpt, "The Kitten and Falling Leaves"*

Tonkinese

Sphinx

Norwegian

Himalayan

Bengal

American Curl

CATS AROUND

Singapura

Turkish Angora

Siam

Chartreux

Ocicat

Oriental Shorthair

Birman

THE WORLD

Photographer's Profile

Yoneo Morita is well known in Japan for his adorable photographs of puppies and kittens. He uses a technique called *hanadeka* ("big nose"), which is widely employed in Japanese iconography. This technique shrinks the animal's body in relation to its nose. Morita is the author of *Utterly Adorable Cats* and *Utterly Loveable Dogs*. He lives in Japan.